creepy creatures

CONTENTS

Published by Creative Education
P.O. Box 227, Mankato, Minnesota 56002
Creative Education is an imprint of
The Creative Company
www.thecreativecompany.us

Design and production by Ellen Huber
Art direction by Rita Marshall
Printed by Corporate Graphics
in the United States of America

Photographs by 123RF (Alle, Edite Artmann, Lucian
Coman, Adrian Hillman, Pavel Konovalov, Le Do),
iStockphoto (Evgeniy Ayupov, Eric Isselée, Bruce
MacQueen, Alan Merrigan, Artiom Muhaciov, Petr
Podzemny, Nico Smit, Mike Sonnenberg, Tomasz
Zachariasz), Shutterstock (Heintje Joseph T. Lee,
orionmystery@flickr)

Library of Congress Cataloging-in-Publication Data
Bodden, Valerie.
Crickets / by Valerie Bodden.
p. cm. — (Creepy creatures)
Summary: A basic introduction to crickets, examining
where they live, how they grow, what they eat, and
the unique traits that help to define them, such as
their ability to chirp or "sing."
Includes index.
ISBN 978-1-58341-993-9
1. Crickets—Juvenile literature. I. Title. II. Series.
QL508.G8B63 2011
595.7'26—dc22   2009052519

CPSIA: 031412 PO1557
9 8 7 6 5 4

crickets

VALERIE BODDEN

CREATIVE EDUCATION

You are outside on a dark summer night. You hear strange music that seems to come from the grass. What could it be? It is the sound of crickets chirping!

chirp chirp chirp

Crickets are **insects**. Their bodies have three main parts. A cricket's head has two long, thin **antennae** (*an-TEH-nee*) on top. Sometimes the antennae are longer than the cricket's body!

Crickets use their antennae to feel and touch things

Crickets have six legs. The back legs are very strong. They help crickets jump far! Most crickets have wings, too. Crickets are usually brown or black.

Most crickets are between half an inch and two inches (1.25–5 cm) long.

Some crickets that live in trees are a light green color

Some ground crickets have a very hard outer shell

There are about 2,000 different kinds of crickets. Field crickets can be found in many places. House crickets and ground crickets are common, too.

Crickets live all around the world. They make their homes in meadows, forests, and deserts. Some even live in people's houses! Crickets have to watch out for **predators**. Spiders, snakes, and lizards called chameleons (*kuh-MEEL-yunz*) all eat crickets.

Chameleons are lizards that can change colors

Mother crickets lay their eggs on the ground or inside plants. Baby crickets are called nymphs (*NIMFS*). Nymphs look like small adult crickets. But they do not have wings. As they grow, the nymphs get too big for their skin. They **molt** so they can keep growing. The crickets grow wings, too. Most crickets live only a few months.

Baby crickets spend a lot of time on or eating plants

Crickets hide during the day. At night, they come out to eat. Crickets eat both plants and insects. Some even eat other crickets!

Some ground crickets eat other crickets that have died

A male's calling song is made up of a few short chirps

Male crickets can make pretty music. They rub their wings together to "sing." Their singing **attracts** females. The females hear the sound through hearing **organs** on their legs.

People sometimes carry crickets with them for good luck

Some people keep pet crickets in cages. They might even enter their pets in singing contests! Other people think that crickets are good luck. It can be fun finding and watching these musical creepy creatures!

MAKE A CRICKET'S SONG

To "sing," crickets rub the edge of one wing against a ridge on the other wing. You can sing like a cricket, too. All you need is a comb and a stick. Hold the comb in one hand. Rub the stick back and forth across the teeth of the comb. Try rubbing the stick faster and slower. Does the sound of your song change?

GLOSSARY

antennae: feelers on the heads of some bugs that are used to touch, smell, and taste things

attracts: gets another animal to pay attention or come closer

insects: small animals with three body parts and six legs; most have two pairs of wings, too

molt: to lose a shell or layer of skin and grow a new, larger one

organs: body parts that do certain jobs; for example, eyes are organs for seeing

predators: animals that kill and eat other animals

READ MORE

Green, Emily. *Crickets*. Minneapolis: Bellwether Media, 2007.

Meister, Cari. *Crickets*. Edina, Minn.: Abdo Publishing, 2001.

WEB SITES

Enchanted Learning: Cricket

http://www.enchantedlearning.com/subjects/insects/orthoptera/Cricket.shtml

Learn more about crickets and print a cricket picture to color.

Insecta Inspecta World: Field Crickets

http://www.insecta-inspecta.com/crickets/field/index.html

Read about crickets and listen to the sound of crickets chirping.

INDEX